iNSPYRe Me

CAREGIVER GUIDE

IT IS WIDELY BELIEVED THAT BETWEEN THE AGES OF 0 - 5 YEARS AN INFANT IS ESSENTIALLY A SPONGE. THAT IS TO SAY THAT EVERYTHING THEY HEAR, SEE, AND EXPERIENCE GOES DIRECTLY INTO THEIR SUBCONSCIOUS MIND AND BECOMES A PART OF THEIR LIFELONG PERSPECTIVE, OR PARADIGM.

"BABY'S FIRST AFFIRMATIONS" IS DESIGNED TO ENSURE THAT POSITIVE STATEMENTS ARE REPEATED AND INGRAINED IN THE SUBCONSCIOUS MIND FROM THE VERY BEGINNING, THEREBY ALLOWING POSITIVE PERSPECTIVES/SELF-IMAGES TO GROW WITH THEM THROUGHOUT LIFE.

THIS BOOK USES THE GENERAL TERM 'YOU', PLEASE FEEL FREE TO ADD THE BABY'S NAME TO MAKE AN EVEN STRONGER IMPRESSION. EX: "YOU, CHLOE, ARE CREATIVE" OR; "YOU, ALEC, ARE HEALTHY."

READ THIS BOOK TO THEM OFTEN. THROUGHOUT THE DAY REPEAT THE WORDS IN GENERAL SPEECH, RE-AFFIRMING THE POSITIVE QUALITIES YOU WANT THEM TO GROW-UP BELIEVING ABOUT THEMSELVES.

iNSPYre me IS ABOUT CREATING POSITIVE BELIEFS AND ATTITUDES IN EVERYONE, YOUNG AND OLD ALIKE.

THE INSPYRE ME COLLECTION: FOR A POSITIVE START TO LIFE.

You are
HAPPY!

You are
LOVED!

You are
STRONG.

You are
HEALTHY

You are
KIND

You are

INTELLIGENT

You are

CREATIVE!

You are

PLAYFUL!

You are
WORTHY

You are

INFINITE.

INSPYRE ME

Made in the USA
Middletown, DE
12 January 2023

22037430R00015